FutureWord Publishing

Settle for Best: Satisfy the Winner You Were Born to Be

© 2012 by Kristine M. Smith   **All rights reserved.**

ISBN: **9780615639000** First print edition 07.07.2012
Cover Design by C.S. Trent, Din Faction

This book is printed in the USA
www.FutureWord.net

07.07.12

SETTLE

FOR

BEST

SATISFY THE WINNER YOU WERE BORN TO BE

Kristine M. Smith

PRAISE FOR **SETTLE FOR BEST**

"I've just read a pre-publication copy of *SETTLE FOR BEST: Satisfy the Winner You Were Born to Be* by Kristine M Smith. This is a valuable reference book, infused with the author's signature lively use of the English language. It sure helped me in my current challenge!" —Edward E Smith, Yelm, Washington.

Settle For Best: Satisfy the Winner You Were Born to Be by Kristine M Smith is a delightfully good read for people who want to improve themselves or find their inner happiness. This book is invaluable, jam packed with Kris's zest and love for life and how she is willing to share it with the world. Like her mentor (and my inspiration) DeForest Kelley did for me with the show he was in (Star Trek) and the way he looked at and lived his life, Kristine's new book has helped me put life's challenges in a new light and, along with De Kelley, has re-sparked *my* zest and love for life and my commitment to reaching my goals. Can't wait 'till it hits the shelves— Greg Barton, Australia

"Kristine M. Smith's motivational book has strength of content and style, salted with wit and humor. The informal, personal and expressive style gives the reader comfort and encouragement to explore new ideas and goals. Settle for Best has the mark of a classic and will benefit ALL who read it." — Walter and Karen Dobbs SeaTac, Washington

"I very much enjoyed *Settle for Best*. An easy read, it is educational and inspiring. Our motto at the Small Business Training Center is 'Knowledge is Money'. This is a must-read if prosperity is your goal." — Garry Stutz, Small Business Training Center

"I found this book positively inspirational. The contents and presentation are stellar. The author, Kristine M Smith, shares her life experiences as she offers sage advice about how to transform dreams into realities. It's a step-by-step process; it takes work and determination, but it's ours to have if we have the nerve to take the first step and the persistence to continue with the steps that follow.

"The Table of Contents lays out the author's method clearly. In fact, I found each chapter able to stand on its own. The second chapter is "Be Positive and Passionate—two key words that explain one of the steps in a nutshell. The chapter title says it all, but the real wisdom is gleaned from reading the chapter. It's such an important point. The author's keys to success are based on keeping ourselves focused on our personal desires. Using the strategies she provides can lead to success in business and other life pursuits.

"It's certainly worked for Kris! I don't personally know anyone with greater drive and determination. This formula for success has proven to be effective for her and has led to great results. What a great journey she's on! I've known Kris since 1981 and have watched her work on and realize her goals with my own eyes. This is her seventh book in just ten years. All of them are great reads and each one is as different as you can get topic-wise. I've been delighted and elevated by every one of them. Like the pastor she quotes in this book, Kris wants to "die empty," having done everything on her Bucket List she wants to do as a writer. I can't wait for her next creation."
—Nancy Graf, Retired High School teacher

CONTENTS

Foreword 11

My Story—How Much of It is Yours, Too? 15

What Millionaires Do that Others Don't 23

It Takes DESIRE to Focus on Your Goals 27

Plan Your Work and Work Your Plan 31

Never Lose Your Childlike Desire for Abundant Life 35

Ignore Naysayers 41

Visualize Completed Goals..................................45

Train Your Subconscious Mind 49

Build Coalitions (Cohesive Specialization)........53

Remain a Life-long Learner 57

Decide Quickly, Change Your Mind Slowly.......61

Persist 65

Access Infinite Intelligence 69

Use Your Faith Consistently 73

Don't Fear Failure 77

Don't Fear Success 81

Love What You Do..85

Consider Setbacks Temporary...........................91

Have a "Significant Other" Who Inspires You....95

Realize Goals are Magnetic 99

Be Positive and Passionate 103

Foster a Success-Conscious Mindset 107

Recognize the True Value of Your Goals 109

In Conclusion: Don't Settle for Less! 117

Note from Publisher 121

FOREWORD

I'm one happy woman. I'm not rich—by a long shot! I'm not svelte. I'm not super smart or terribly outstanding in any other way. (Others have disagreed on these last points. I'm happy to disagree with their disagreement!)

Although I've always had a happy, hopeful nature, I've had a tough row to hoe. Still, inside every unhappy moment, I've always known there's more than what's happening right now in the wee corners of my circumstances.

I vibrate to possibility. I dance to the delight of knowing that the only person who can defeat me is me.

And I've defeated myself plenty of times.

My story is probably much like yours. The difference is this: I've achieved my breakthrough. If you're still looking for yours, this is a good place to start.

You _can_ achieve your dreams no matter how high the hill you have to climb to get there...but you have to put schedules and "due dates" on them. You have to transform your thoughts into achievable, step-by-step goals.

Unless you do, someday—not long from now—you'll be sadly pondering why you're "suddenly" old and feeling like you'd kill for a "do over" _if only_ you could turn back time.

I'm giving you that chance...in advance. Will you take it?

"Our deepest fear is not that we are inadequate. Our deepest fear is that we are powerful beyond measure. It is our light, not our darkness that most frightens us. We ask ourselves, 'Who am I to be brilliant, gorgeous, talented, fabulous?' Actually, who are you not to be? You are a child of God. Your playing small does not serve the world. There is nothing enlightened about shrinking so that other people won't feel insecure around you.

We are all meant to shine, as children do. We were born to make manifest the glory of God that is within us. It's not just in some of us; it's in everyone. And as we let our own light shine, we unconsciously give other people permission to do the same. As we are liberated from our own fear, our presence automatically liberates others."

— Marianne Williamson

CHAPTER ONE

My Story—How Much of It is Yours, Too?

I was born into a working class family. My dad, an unwanted child, had a sixth grade education, a verbally and physically abusive father, and a drinking problem. Despite his circumstances, he achieved far beyond what most other folks would have anticipated to be his fate. He made millions. He also squandered them. His decision to persist despite his shortcomings is the engine that assured his success.

My father's forte was construction. He started as a bricklayer's apprentice, absorbing everything he learned while at work. Over time he transformed himself and became a much-in-demand general contractor. He built part of the Washington State Library in Olympia, Tacoma General Hospital, slews of homes, and many of the brand name restaurants you see all over the country.

Living under his roof was a trial to his children and wife. He was verbally abusive, demanding, and criminally unsympathetic to our desires to do anything other than what he wanted us to do. I was suspect because I wanted to become a writer. He wasn't even a reader. Unless we were all doing what he wanted, we were being "lazy." And he "analyzed" *to death* beforehand every chore we were given, making *this* kid resentful before I ever set foot out the door to "get 'er done!"

My mom—although a voracious reader—didn't support my desire to become a writer either. Back then, there wasn't the demand for writers that there is today, thanks to cable stations, the Internet, and other inventions unforeseeable in her day. Mom was sure I would starve to death unless I became well-versed in a "real" career that would support me reliably. So I dutifully became a secretary/ administrative assistant.

Back then, I figured they were both right! My dad was right because I **was** unenthusiastic to the max when it came to doing things I absolutely hated, so I rushed through them like Grant took Richmond just to finish them so I could open up space in my life to write. Dad considered this "laziness." I considered it super efficiency: do what you *gotta* do fast so you can get to what you *wanna* do faster! My mom was right because only James Michener, Leon Uris, Louis L'Amour, and a handful of other writers were making a decent living back then.

But this "writing thing" just **would not** let me go! As unpromising as it was at the time, it was my "drug," my addiction, my passion. So I kept writing; I have literally hundreds of journals to prove it.

Malcolm Gladwell writes in *The Tipping Point,* that to become an expert in any field, it's necessary to invest ten thousand hours in the pursuit. I'd far exceeded ten thousand hours of writing time by the time I was eighteen years old. Strangely enough, my first nationally-published article happened at eighteen, thanks to actor DeForest Kelley who shared the manuscript with a national TV magazine in New York. They wanted to publish it. I was over the moon! Mr. Kelley remained an enthusiastic encourager until his death in 1999. (You can read more about my association with Mr. Kelley in ***DeForest Kelley: A Harvest of Memories.***)

English and Creative Writing teachers, Mrs. Choyce, Alpha Rossetti, and Walter Dobbs also encouraged me, but...silly me...back then, it was the naysayers in my life—my parents—I listened to most and regarded as "knowing me and my potential best." **WRONG!!!!** Hear me, loud and clear: Naysayers are the blight on too many horizons. **Never** consider naysayers wise counsel. As long as other people, in better positions to know about your potential, encourage you, *keep going*!

I've invested thousands of dollars and tens of thousands of hours reading self-help books. I did this because I was unhappy as a 9-to-5 secretary and knew I wasn't cut out for it, **even though I was very good at it.**

There's a passage in the Bible that reads, *"Raise up a child in the way he should go and when he is old he will not depart from it"* (Proverbs 22:6).

I always thought that meant, "Raise up a good little Christian or Jew and when he is old, he will remain one." What it actually means is, "Find out what your wee one's passion is, and as long as it can serve others, encourage him to pursue it by giving him the encouragement, knowledge, and skills he needs to succeed as a businessman later in life doing what he loves." WOW! What a HUGE difference a little excavation of the Scriptures makes!

Too many parents are sending their unique, creative, enthusiastic, gung-ho kids to cookie-cutter schools that raise cookie-cutter citizens. Why? Fear! They're afraid that if their kids don't toe the line, stick with the straight-and-narrow, they'll fight poverty for the rest of their lives.

But what about the poverty of spirit they'll have if they're herded into careers that don't excite them? What about the poverty of contribution when they do show up only to put in the minimum effort required to collect their next paycheck? Employees who "check out" on arrival are parasites, party poopers, not positive contributors to a cause.

Parents: don't feel guilty! You were *taught* to think this way! It's unnatural **not** to worry about your children's long-term survival. Part of your job description as a parent is to counsel wisely and gently guide your children to self-sufficiency.

The problem happens when we start looking at job market projections and steering our kids to the careers most likely to need lots of warm bodies for the foreseeable future. Not everyone is cut out to be a medical worker, IT engineer, or an alternate energy expert. Imagine, just for a brief moment—so you don't let your imagination spoil your day— lying helplessly in a hospital bed being monitored by a person who couldn't care less about you, your comfort, or your well-being. "Hey, they needed nurses, so I became a nurse..."

Nurses are special people. They SHOULD be special people. Not everyone can handle the constant pressure of holding other people's lives in their hands.

The same goes for teachers, plumbers, writers, actors, singers, musicians, bankers, and electricians. It takes a unique passion to carry the torch for an extended period of time in any field. Those without passion for what they do burn out long before they wear out.

People come in all "flavors": extroverted, introverted, and perverted! Expecting an introverted wallflower to excel on the sales floor is insanity taken to the ninth power. Expecting an extrovert to sit in a cubicle and crunch numbers all day is equally nuts.

If all this is making sense to you, you're in the right place. Because whatever your passion is, there's a niche for you in this world. You no longer have to "fit in" to survive. You have the option of standing out and thriving, even as an introverted wallflower.

It isn't easy. Stop reading now if you expect success to come as quickly and easily as you can order up a meal at a drive-thru restaurant.

As my publisher loves to say, "There's a big difference between being 'led beside still waters' and sitting around the watering hole waiting to be fed and quenched. Wherever we stay in our minds is where we live. Live in the upper stratosphere. The fruit of the spirit grows and thrives there."

In the next chapter, I'll define what it takes to succeed.

CHAPTER TWO

What Millionaires Do that Others Don't

In a venerated book, *Think and Grow Rich,* author Napoleon Hill danced all around "the secret" of becoming rich—financially, spiritually, relationally, emotionally. He wrote the book just as America was emerging from the wreckage wrought by the Great Depression. In it, he explored why there are always tens of millions of poverty-stricken souls in a land that regularly spawns multi-millionaires in every kind of economic situation.

Hill interviewed and/or studied Andrew Carnegie, Charles Schwab, Thomas Edison, George Eastman, Teddy Roosevelt, F.W. Woolworth, Luther Burbank, Clarence Darrow, Wilbur Wright, J.D. Rockefeller, Henry Ford, and other giants on his mission to discern which aspects of their personalities and/or practices allowed them to prosper despite working-class beginnings. What he discovered fed him for the rest of his life.

Millionaires come from all walks of life: educated and uneducated; right-brained (writers, actors, poets, etc.) and left-brained (analysts, scientists, etc.); introverted and extroverted. But there is a list of personal assets and attributes that defines all of them. Napoleon Hill defined them:

Successful Millionaires ...

- ➢ Focus fiercely on their goals (desire)
- ➢ Plan their work and work their plan
- ➢ Never lose their childlike desire for abundant life
- ➢ Ignore Naysayers
- ➢ Visualize completed goals before and while   actualizing them
- ➢ Train their subconscious minds to overcome unhelpful thinking
- ➢ Build coalitions of kindred, proactive partners (cohesive specialization)
- ➢ Remain lifelong learners
- ➢ Decide quickly, change their minds slowly
- ➢ Persist
- ➢ Access infinite intelligence via the sixth sense
- ➢ Use their faith the way world-class bodybuilders use weights: consistently
- ➢ Are not afraid of failure
- ➢ Are not afraid of success

- ➤ Love what they do
- ➤ Consider setbacks temporary, not reasons to quit
- ➤ Have a "significant other" who inspires them to keep on keepin' on
- ➤ Know goals are magnetic and genuinely exude the right attitudes and characteristics to attract the essentials needed to achieve them
- ➤ Are positive and passionate
- ➤ Have success-conscious mindsets
- ➤ Recognize the true value of their goals

The above list will work wonders in any area of your life—financial, physical, spiritual, and emotional—so if you're not particularly interested in learning these ideas for monetary reward, you'll still find value in them when pursuing anything else you consider worthwhile in life. But because so many people are seeking more money, I'm going to concentrate on this part of the puzzle. And once you put the pieces together and have the whole picture, you can piece together any picture you want in other areas of your life using the same blueprint.

Look at the list again. Do you see areas where you're not quite up to speed? If so, put a check mark next to them or run a highlighter through them; this way, you'll know which of the following chapters to "zone in" on to complete your repertoire.

CHAPTER THREE

It Takes DESIRE to Focus Fiercely on Your Goals

The difference between a daydream and a definite, do-able goal is unquenchable desire. If you're completely satisfied simply dreaming "what if…," you won't achieve anything more. The dream itself will be adequate.

When what you want is insatiable, unquenchable, irresistible, you're where you must be, mindset-wise, to pursue and attain it. What you want has to compel you through challenges, setbacks, roadblocks, financial hardships, and the whispered worry and skepticism of family, friends, and associates.

What is Desire?

If you've ever been "in love," you know what I'm talking about. In Disney terms, like the teen-age Bambi, you're "twitter-pated." You can't eat, sleep, bathe, work, or play without thinking of your beloved. You're obsessed, possessed!

Confession Time: The reason I've never become rich is because the "money chase" only motivates me passionately when I'm running on fumes financially. I realize, now—belatedly—that this is a risky way to live, so these days I'm money-minded every day...not because I want to be rich, but because I definitely don't want to continue existing just above the poverty line for the rest of my life!

Up until now what has motivated me, and motivates me still, is stringing words together. When I'm writing, I'm deliriously happy, and because of this, I decided to hang my shingle five years ago and dedicate my waking hours to writing for a living. It has been slow going; it has been scary at times, risky for sure...but I feel more alive than I have at any other time in my life. I'm doing what I was meant to do.

If there's something you simply MUST do—something you'd do for free if you weren't compelled to earn money to survive—something that can help others in their lives—*that's* your gift to the world. That's where your legacy lies.

For some, it's being a parent. Trust me, being a parent is *the* quintessential Never-ending Story. You never outgrow or get over it, even after the kids fly the coop. Without intense desire, successful parenting would be impossible because there are lots of trials, setbacks, frustrations, obstacles and heartaches that come with the desire. For others, it's being an engineer, a fireman, a policeman, a writer, a nurse or doctor, or an actor.

Get Up! Get Going!

Don't sit on your asset! Turn your desire into definite, achievable plans and goals. If you're just starting out and still need to put in the requisite ten thousand hours getting your sea legs under you, start today.

Do something every day that advances you. Make it your mission to improve, network, assimilate, and enjoy the steps you're taking.

CHAPTER FOUR

Plan Your Work and Work Your Plan

"The carpenter's standard protocol, 'Measure twice, cut once' rings true in nearly every profession." K.M. Smith

Successful people create a mind map before they set to work on worthwhile projects and courses of action. They make a list of what they have on hand and what they still need to find or buy to realize their goal. They leave no stone unturned; they consult experts and other successful people who have traveled the same road and know where the switchbacks, canyons, and other hazards are located.

Read books on the pursuit that captures your imagination and propels you forward. Pick up the phone or jot an email and ask questions. Imagine every step along the way and consider what might go wrong and how you can fix it if it does go wrong.

Yeah, I know, this takes time. But it usually takes far less time, money, and pain to plan ahead than it does to crash into unanticipated perils on a dark road and end up in the ditch.

Do you have ample money, time, and resources to begin the project? By ample, I mean more than the minimum required, because nothing ever goes exactly according to plan.

If you don't have enough, you've hit your first snag. But guess what? You can handle snags. Take a deep breath, center yourself, and calmly find creative ways to untangle yourself; the sense of satisfaction you'll get will propel you to new heights and a greater sense of self-actualization and confidence. There are always ways over, under, around, or through obstacles if you're on the right path...and you already know you are or you wouldn't be reading this.

Take this to heart: if what you're planning to do were easy, everybody would be doing it. You're made of stern stuff; you have what it takes to tackle the tasks that are required to put the puzzle together and show it to the world as a finished work of art. You can handle the hiccups too. Expect them; they'll happen!

As a copywriter, I live a "feast or famine" existence. It's part of life until I develop enough long-term "regulars" that I no longer have to take the time to look for additional projects to keep me busy. And, in truth, what I've just described will never happen—regulars retire, pass away, or become ill. Or they find someone "better" (a subjective word) or—in some cases—just less expensive because they don't need an uncompromising copywriter to sell what they're offering.

The creative life *is* risky; no two ways about it. But the rewards—chief among them loving what I do—outweigh the risks for me. I have to admit that my complete trust in God's providence also makes my career seem less risky than a non-believer might experience. During "famine" times, He has always come through just in the nick of time, even when I think He should have been quicker on the uptake! But each time it happens, I know I'll be just that much more relaxed and faith-filled *the next time* it happens. I've always been rewarded for my faith in this "exciting" —formerly nerve-wracking!—way, so I experience my relationship with God these days as palpably real and extremely warm. My Heavenly Father takes superb care of me!

CHAPTER FIVE

Never Lose Your Childlike Desire for Abundant Life

If it has been a while since you've watched toddlers playing, visit a pre-school or playground and watch the situation carefully. What do you notice?

Very Young Kids are Un-self-conscious

Children *live* their dreams and invest totally in their imaginations. They have no fear. They explore every aspect of their imaginary realms. They never worry about doing something wrong. It's "their" world, lock, stock, and barrel.

As we grow, various conventions get introduced into our lives: we learn manners, patience, sharing, and compassion. We also learn things that begin to cripple us. We learn to discern whether we're being celebrated or merely tolerated. We begin to regard ourselves as deficient in some ways and proficient in others. We begin to judge ourselves and others.

Although it's necessary to foster discernment, often the lesson is poorly expressed by exasperated, tired adults. Since there is no definitive guide to perfect parenting, some moms and dads—and teachers, too—correct their children in ways that indicate to a child that he or she has become a burden or blight in an otherwise-happy situation.

Before too long, children who begin to consider themselves better off "seen and not heard" retreat from life. Instead of engaging whole-heartedly as they did in earlier, un-self-conscious times, they wait in the shadows, hoping for a kind word or gentle encouragement to join activities.

It goes without saying that children who don't feel they "fit in," begin to check out and build walls of their own making to keep out the hurt of reproach, which they translate as rejection. All of them are hopeful, passionate, intelligent, creative kids. They just no longer want to risk standing out, because being who they are appears frowned upon.

Sound familiar? Am I writing your biography here? I'm reciting my own! We're the Walking Wounded—people who, as kids, were told we were somehow "missing the target" in Mom's and Dad's well-ordered world. *It hurt!* We may still be living with the legacy of that laceration. I know I did for a very long time!

Here's the Truth about You

➤ You are a one-of-a-kind wonder! You always **have** been; you *always will* be! Whatever someone told you about yourself that hurt you when you were little, you're free to disregard now.

➤ If you were deemed an alien in your own family, it was your parents' responsibility—not yours—to discern what you had to offer the world that they *couldn't* offer because they were created to offer something else.

➢ God doesn't make junk. The Universal Mind doesn't make junk: everything in existence serves a unique purpose.

Your assignment: Talk to the injured child within you. Let him/her know that YOU know the truth about what an amazing human being God made. Your assignment is to take him/her by the hand back to the time BEFORE damage was done by imprecise, unskillfully-shared remarks. Watch as he plays again un-self-consciously and with complete abandon. Memorize the body language of full-out participation in life. Let your child know she is beautiful and that she has great gifts to offer the world.

Your desire to release your wounded inner child from bondage will compel you to repeat this assignment until you see her/him all grown up and interacting with life in the same way she/he did as an undamaged wee one.

Free people free others to be themselves. And only truly free people leave legacies that inspire untold generations.

Want to influence the world—or just your part of it? Be yourself! You can only be a second-rate someone else, so corner the market on being yourself and watch what happens.

CHAPTER SIX

Ignore Naysayers

"How many naysayers—in their lives—are where you want to be in yours?" — **Kristine M. Smith**

Have you noticed how much the naysayers in your life have in common? I have.

Their lives don't resemble anything I want to make of my life.

- ❖ They seem to be afraid, angry, apathetic, depressed, or arrogant.
- ❖ They say they're just being "realistic" as they "burst your bubble."
- ❖ They go along to get along.
- ❖ They don't applaud when you do something extraordinary.
- ❖ They don't seem to be (personally) extraordinary themselves.
- ❖ They're sourpusses.

Why would you give away your power to someone like that?

Naysayers don't expect to win, don't want you to win, and don't applaud when you do win. Why? You're a living contradiction to their world view. They see you as someone who is certainly "no better than they are" and yet...and yet... "somehow" you make it—and they feel personally cheated. They tell others (maybe even you) that you "got lucky." You "had advantages" they didn't have. You "were self-centered and addicted to your goal."

God forbid you should win! What your win says to them is that they lost, even though they were every bit as "qualified" to win as you are.

And they're right! They were! Except for one thing: They elected to sit on their assets and rust in place while you—like **The Little Engine that Could**—kept chugging forward up mountainsides telling yourself, "I think I can, I think I can, I think I can..." until you DID!

There is no secret to most peoples' success. It's the folks who get up every morning with a positive attitude, a list of goals with deadlines on them, and a sense of their own destiny, who meet the challenges, negotiate the roadblocks, and end up where they want to be. Naysayers need not apply.

Henry Ford had it exactly right. "Whether you think you can or think you can't, you're right."

So the next time you hear from a naysayer, be kind. Just don't be so kind that you cripple yourself by taking their counsel to heart. Feel sorry for them, not for yourself. They've adopted a world view that hamstrings them, on the outside of possibilities, no longer even looking in. They don't know how dead their spirits are. Someone clobbered them at a very young age with "realistic" perspectives, attitudes, and (say it loud and say it proud) limitations. They're limited to what they think is "likely" instead of pursuing what is entirely possible.

Realistic people rarely make history. It's the folks who know things can always be better who change the world.

If there's a persistent, persnickety naysayer in your life, you may have to bite the bullet and say goodbye to him or her. That, too, will be expected. Naysayers know they're a drag on your spirit; they just can't seem to help themselves. They're afraid for you, afraid for themselves. The possibility of you building a new life and real success frightens them. They feel comfortable right where they are, right where you are.

This may not seem to make sense to you, but it makes perfect sense to them. Naysayers want to be right; they're rarely happy when proven wrong.

CHAPTER SEVEN

Visualize Completed Goals Before and While Actualizing Them

"From a very early age, I knew I would be a writer; I felt it in my bones." — Kristine M. Smith

Successful people "see the end from the beginning," not as some sort of cloudy daydream or beckoning mirage but as a "done deal." They "watch" their future selves walking in success.

In my case, I visualized myself signing copies of my books, talking easily with fans (*that* was the greatest stretch, as shy as I was), *and* taking my royalties and book sales to the bank and depositing them.

That's probably why every professional service I provided, until I became an author and copywriter, assaulted my spirit to one degree or another. I was very good as an executive secretary and administrative assistant—don't get me wrong! I performed my duties. I was uniformly cheerful, helpful, and passionate about helping my employers succeed; they were good people whose passion for their goals matched my own. They were making things happen, and I was grateful to be deemed competent to be on their teams!

But I was working **their** dreams and goals, not my own. It wasn't the same. I knew why I was put here on God's green earth; there was never a doubt in my mind. I wanted to string words together and make things **happen** in the same way God spoke the world into motion. I was (still am) in love with the power of words. They transform. They change things.

"The pen is mightier than the sword." - Edward Bulwer-Lytton

"Nothing can withstand the power of an idea whose time has come." – Victor Hugo

If you want something so badly that you've been "seeing" it for years as a "done deal," you're in a good place. But if you have a passion to succeed in a role that *isn't* as cemented into the vision of your future, start where you are: begin to touch, taste, see, and feel what it will be like **when** —not if—you succeed.

If you recognize aspects of your visualized future that go against your grain (e.g., my anxiety about interacting with fans of my books), do whatever it takes to begin to overcome the tension you feel about that aspect of your future, or it **will** slow you down— it did me! I took public speaking and debate classes as a teen and adult; later on, I imagined myself interacting with strangers as easily as I interacted with the folks I served while performing my duties as an executive secretary and administrative assistant. I "acted as if" I wasn't shy, or hesitant; in this way, I out-witted my "wallflower" persona. Today, people laugh when I confess to shyness. ***"You?! Shy?!!! BWAAAA-HA-HA-HA-HA-HA"*** Oddly enough, other shy people who have worked mightily on the same handicap recognize right away that I'm a kindred spirit who has managed to triumph anyway by walking through the fear.

It is those with the ability to visualize their goals as "done deals" in every detail, and who come to grips ahead of time with the less-rosy aspects of their future success who develop the stamina and determination to push through the setbacks and obstacles that line every road to their future reality.

Before you retire every night, visualize what your future will hold when you get where you're going. See what you're able to do then, and who's walking with you, helping you, applauding you, and helping you make things happen. Then put your visualization into action. Make your daily to-do list a reflection (or a precursor, if you will) of the future you expect to inhabit. Talk **now** to the folks you'll be serving when you get where you're going. Talk **now** to the folks who can help you get where you're going. Mentors are everywhere, and good mentors *love* being considered your go-to-experts.

Visualize what you want, then assemble the puzzle pieces that will carry you there.

CHAPTER EIGHT

Train Your Subconscious Mind to Overcome Unhelpful Thinking

Your subconscious mind is miraculous. It pumps your heart, circulates your blood, regulates your breathing, stimulates your nerves in response to internal and external stimuli, and much, much more without you even having to think about it.

Until you were seven or eight years old, you operated primarily from your subconscious mind. Your brain was like a sponge, absorbing everything within your environment without judging or blocking a stitch of it.

It is the inability of the subconscious mind to recognize helpful and unhelpful messages that is its chief drawback. Are you familiar with the following lesson?

Children Learn What They Live
By Dorothy Law Nolte, Ph.D.

If children live with criticism, they learn to condemn.

If children live with hostility, they learn to fight.

If children live with fear, they learn to be apprehensive.

If children live with pity, they learn to feel sorry for themselves.

If children live with ridicule, they learn to feel shy.

If children live with jealousy, they learn to feel envy.

If children live with shame, they learn to feel guilty.

There is more to Nolte's lesson. She says that when children learn positive things from the adults in their lives, they absorb possibility, positivity, and preparation.

It isn't easy to "unlearn" unhelpful lessons from childhood. Sometimes it takes years of counseling to ease the damage that thoughtless adults have done to innocent children. But it can be done.

If you were told by significant adults that you were "daydreaming" when you proclaimed (as a dependent child) that you wanted to be a/an _____ (whatever it is you're seeking to become), it's hard to overcome that. We tend to fulfill our parents' prophecies for us because we figure they know us better than anyone else does. Tellingly, I didn't publish my first book until both of my parents were dead. I dutifully served in lesser roles to make sure they felt secure that I was making a reliable living and that I would be okay financially. I have since written seven books and become a professional copywriter; I make 99 percent of my living as a writer.

If you were told you were lazy because you preferred pursuing your own goals to pursuing a parent's or teacher's, you absorbed that and subscribed to it, and you may now "walk it out" as an adult, agreeing that you're "just too lazy to buckle down and do what it takes to reach my goals."

Do you see how unhelpful personal labels, handed down by clueless adults, may have crippled you?

The good news is this: You're an adult now and you can re-parent and nurture the wounded child inside you. Tell her/him that you recognize the potential and the enthusiasm inside you. Let him/her know that you're 110 percent on the team; you know how to help now.

Don't let yesterday's unhelpful labels keep you stuck. You know better now. Use affirmations that underscore your abilities and willingness to carry the dream to goal-hood and the goal to reality.

You can do this. God doesn't make junk.

CHAPTER NINE

Build Coalitions of Kindred, Proactive Partners (Cohesive Specialization)

One of America's least-helpful myths is the myth of the "self-made man." Rugged individualism may work if you're a cowboy and your plan is to raise, feed, kill, skin, and eat the cattle you raise and then wear their hide atop your own to stay warm during long winter months, but c'mon.... even the Lone Ranger had Tonto!

Too many entrepreneurs are trying to "go it alone" so no one else can tamper with their plans (or perhaps share in their successes). To succeed in the world, you need more than five thousand Facebook friends even if you're blessed enough to have 10 percent or more of them who are "sneezers"—avid fans who can't seem to stop singing your praises. You need strategic partners who will scout out prospects for you, share in your risks, and provide some of the guidance you'll need to make everything work the way it must to keep the ball rolling.

In my case, I have other small business owners who refer clients to me, just as I refer clients to them as I find prospects they can help in a big way. I have a delightful publisher who's also a fan of my stuff, so she's always on the lookout for additional writing for me to do, whether it's editing, ghosting, or critiquing. I have friends and family members who listen for the cry of a business owner who needs a good wordsmith, a retired person, or a gung-ho entrepreneur who realizes there is a lot he or she wants put into book or article form. And I belong to writers' groups because, hey, writers are usually very cool people who know a lot about the human condition, have lots of irons in the fire, and some of them might need an occasional assist if they get over-booked and want to off-load projects without dropping their standards of excellence.

If the above sounds like "You scratch my back and I'll scratch yours," that's too cut-and-dried. It isn't about "getting" all the time—or even much of the time. It's about getting to know others and "trading" with them whenever you realize they can help one of your clients better than you can in one or more instances. There's no shame in that.

To the degree that you **don't** network to find strategic partners while helping others fulfill their own goals, you will not succeed. People who play well together usually get farther and have a lot more fun getting there than do those who try to make magic all on their own. It's called **synergy**, baby: *"the working together of two or more people, organizations, or things, especially when the result is greater than the sum of their individual effects or capabilities!"*

Jesus is the only man who walked on water without help; the rest of us need a motorboat and water skis to stay up there—and some of us need more than that to stay on those pernicious slats of fiberglass!

Find Complementary-but-Kindred Collaborators

If you're a writer, published or unpublished, find a graphics designer/webmaster whose work you love and whose personality and passion for what he or she does meets or exceeds your own.

If you're a realtor, find a mortgage broker, a great sales writer, and any other specialists who will help you do what you do best.

If you flip fixer-upper properties, find banks willing to help you and a writer willing to tout your services.

Every business owner should know a great business card expert, webmaster, apps developer, and copywriter personally. (In case you haven't noticed, I believe every business can benefit from the services of a great wordsmith.)

Whatever it is you offer, think of related non-competitors who can "close the circle" so that when your client needs more than you offer, you are ready to recommend someone you know who will do a great job for them. When you do this, you gain their trust and loyalty, and they'll refer others to you who are in need of wisdom and help like yours.

CHAPTER TEN

Remain a Life-long Learner

"Everybody is a genius. But if you judge a fish by its ability to climb a tree, it will spend its life thinking it's stupid." — Albert Einstein

Successful people are voracious learners; they never stop accumulating knowledge; they're always hungry for more insights. Does this describe you? If not— you're at a distinct disadvantage. But there's hope. Read on!

It's time to uncover **why** you're actively opposed to learning more.

> ➤ Hint: It probably goes back to your school days. (Read Chapter Eight, *Train Your Subconscious Mind to Overcome Unhelpful Thinking* and Chapter Six, *Ignore Naysayers*, if you haven't already.)
> ➤ Were you told as a student that you were "just average in the brains department" by a significant adult (parent, other relative, or teacher)?

- ➢ Were you told you were "lazy, unmotivated, hopeless" as a mover-and-shaker because you didn't ask, "How high?" when the adults in your life told you to jump?
- ➢ Are you a hesitant or sub-par reader?

Read the first line of the quote that begins this chapter. Read it five times. Memorize it. Now go to a mirror and quote the first line while you look into the mirror. (Go ahead. I'll wait.)

Did you do it? Now do it again. ***Repeat it until you believe it***.

You are a genius. Couple your genius to your passion and you'll win. Don't let anyone else's unhelpful negative opinion of you—or your own—derail you.

If you're a fish, it's okay to stop trying to climb that darned tree. So stop. Look for the water you were made to swim in and dive in. Notice how effortless it feels; even when things get a little dicey, it never feels as bad as it did trying to climb that freakin' tree!

NOW when you read a book, watch a video, or ask a question, it will be about learning to swim better in the pond you love. What you learn now will inspire and encourage you. The teachings you assign yourself will make sense to your trajectory, too, so they'll be endlessly fascinating.

And just like that, you've become a lifelong learner—swimming, schooling, and dining with other lifelong learners who are happy to help you, even as you help them.

Suddenly, life takes on brighter hues. The more you learn the better things get.

CHAPTER ELEVEN

Decide Quickly, Change Your Mind Slowly

"Don't worry too much about making the right decision. Just make the decision, and then make the decision right." — Larry Winget

"The most difficult thing is the decision to act; the rest is merely tenacity. Your fears are paper tigers. You can do anything you decide to do. You can act to change and control your life; and the procedure, the process is its own reward." —**Amelia Earhart**

Successful people trust themselves to make good decisions. They intuitively know what can work when they put their energies behind it. Their significant others—partners, employees, spouses, relatives—may disagree; others may even tremble as a decision is made, but successful decision-makers calmly "know" that their course of action is right and that it can and probably will work.

God has a way of bringing "prophetic utterances" about you and me to fruition. To quote Henry Ford again, "Whether you think you can or think you can't, you're right."

Who decided you should be a fish in a tree? Surely it wasn't you, but you honored the prophecy and did your level best to make it happen. And now you're up a tree gasping for water! Dr. Phil would inquire, "How's that workin' for ya?"

You can decide again. You can change your mind and please your spirit instead of obeying the oracle who declared you a tree fish.

You and I get from life what we fervently expect from life. Many people call this the Law of Attraction. The vitality and energy of your true spirit determines your outcome.

Are your hands often clenched into fists? If so, what do you think will be taken away if you un-clench them? What do you think would happen if you opened your hands wide, and with love and thanksgiving, simply accepted what God wants to give you?

If you've made a decision to change course, and you know in your spirit you can make a go of it, then go for it! The only person who can stop you after you've declared your new goal is you.

Naysayers will try; hesitant, co-dependent loved ones will fret. You aren't responsible for their reactions. You <u>are</u> responsible for your future, just as you're responsible for where you are right now. The choices you made, the choices you allowed others to make for you, have brought you to where you are.

Prophesy anew. Prophesy something new, something better.

Decide quickly; change your mind slowly. That's what successful people do, according to Napoleon Hill.

CHAPTER TWELVE

Persist

"Ambition is the path to success. Persistence is the vehicle you arrive in." — **Bill Bradley**

"Flaming enthusiasm, backed up by horse sense and persistence, is the quality that most frequently makes for success." — **Dale Carnegie**

We will never know how many Gold Rush folks quit just inches, minutes, hours, or days before they struck the mother lode. Nor will we know how many of our friends, relatives, and associates called it a day the day before their miracle occurred. All we can know for sure is that one day, they decided they'd had enough and packed it in.

Running water is persistent. It runs into rocks, whittling them down to grains of sand over time. In the Bible, it was the persistence of the widow who kept after the judge that won her what she needed. During the anti-slavery and civil rights movements, it was the persistence of abolitionists and ordinary citizens that eventually thwarted the will of the people who traded in human suffering and privation.

Persistence is the oil that lubricates the gears of success. You can have the best brain, idea, plan, or intention in the world; without persistence, you'll remain powerless and anonymous.

Persistence trumps the commercial static that permeates our capitalistic culture. Persistence out-lasts the severest opposition. It is persistence that has brought me to this page. There were times it would have been easier to have a weekend to myself—but this book was in my brain and wanted OUT!

Whatever it is you're after in life and in business, you have to want it so fiercely that it won't leave you alone. Until it gets done, it pesters you, winks at you, and seduces you. It's like a child who repeatedly tugs on your pants leg and says, "Mommy . . . mommy . . . mommy . . ." until you respond.

You persist when you absolutely must finish something. You persist despite procrastination, poverty, peril, and prosperity. You persist because it's in your DNA. You persist because your goal is bigger than anything else that stands in its path.

CHAPTER THIRTEEN

Access Infinite Intelligence via Your Sixth Sense

There is a part of you that recognizes its universal Source and can access the universal wisdom it finds there. Jesus referred to this innate ability when he proclaimed, *"My sheep know my voice, and I know them, and they follow me"* (John 10:27).

There is a dimension of spirit that recognizes and is compelled to respond to unseen, all-knowing Intelligence. Some people consider the sixth sense the conduit. I would suggest that the true conduit is faith—having extreme faith in the "secret knowing" that beckons you onward to destinations which other people cannot see or comprehend from where they stand.

In our multi-faceted society, many things demand our attention, often against our druthers: loud voices and noises, fast action, invasive ads, jarring music. All of these things, and more, keep most people preoccupied, dealing with their present circumstances. Perhaps this is why so few people "believe in" the sixth sense (their first five senses are "sufficient unto the day" to deal with!) or God/Infinite Intelligence: they've so rarely been exposed to them.

To access Infinite Intelligence and enable your sixth sense, calm is usually necessary, at least until you get good at discerning them in the middle of chaos—calm surroundings and a calm spirit. Pastoral and other natural surroundings are the best conductors. It isn't easy to find these in many places; sometimes it takes driving out into the countryside or to a deserted beach or hilltop.

Successful business people hone their skills in this area to such a degree that they can access Infinite Intelligence and their sixth sense in nearly every kind of environment. Some meditate daily or more often; others "enter the zone" while at their desks simply by opening to what's available to all who are attentive.

It is often said "We are not physical beings experiencing a spiritual life; we are spiritual beings experiencing a physical life." This physical life is so alien to our spirits that it often demands our full attention; learning to walk, talk, and function as temporary beings is time-consuming and often terrifying. Our spirits know that our present bodies have an end date, so we often feel we're wearing egg shells rather than armor.

That's why deciding to do what we came here to do often seems so scary to our physical minds. Our spirits may be urging us, encouraging us, but we drag our feet and back pedal for fear we'll break into pieces and, like Humpty Dumpty, be ruined forever.

Successful people are led by Infinite Intelligence via their sixth sense or complete faith in their abilities to "do all things" that their Source suggests they're capable of doing.

If you've always "known" where you belong in this world as a business person—or in any other role— but you've allowed circumstances and other people to lead you away, now's the time to re-orient yourself and head back in the direction of the Voice you hear: the Voice that assures you that you are here at this exact time to perform specific tasks and actions. You're not a serf or a slave. You're a master (or specially-designed to **become** a master) at something. What is it? Only you can know. Finding your niche and your passion is an inside job. Those who suggest options for you are just guessing based on what they see as your surface assets or on what they want to see you become to satisfy their own druthers. Allow your sixth sense to guide you. Get quiet and begin to listen again to what the Higher Power tells you.

CHAPTER FOURTEEN

Use Your Faith Consistently the Way World-Class Bodybuilders Use Weights

Most of the last chapter talked about accessing Infinite Intelligence via your sixth sense. I added "faith" as another conduit to Infinite Intelligence. Let's pursue this thread further.

Napoleon Hill found that every successful businessman he interviewed consistently used their faith to further their pursuits. Whether Christian, Jewish, Muslim— even atheist or agnostic!—successful businesspeople have faith; perhaps not faith as you or I would define it, but faith nevertheless. To "believe" something is very powerful.

Believe means "to accept as true; **feel sure** of the truth of (something)." When you **believe in** something or someone, you have complete faith in them.

Here's just one example:

When you run in a park and get to a bench where you plan to rest, you have complete faith that it will hold you up when you sit down on it; you **believe in it**. It is only if you see fractures, holes, bench legs askew, and other anomalies that indicate the bench has seen better days and has become **unbelievable** (unsound) that you even think twice about plunking down on it.

Faith is as solid as a park bench to a true believer. Faith is your mother's embrace if you have/had a great mom. **Faith should translate to belief in action. Yours!**

Until you use your faith as reliably as great moms and dads use theirs, or great athletes train their bodies, you will never know how far it can take you.

Do you lack faith in your abilities in *any* of the areas you know you'll have to inhabit as you move forward in life? If so, you may be slowing your own progress. If you feel less adept at certain aspects of what lies ahead, it's okay to get help. I need help with accounting; math and I parted company when New Math came along. I have

ZERO faith in my ability to crunch numbers. So I hire someone whose strength is numbers; I hire someone who has faith in their own abilities to keep me safe and accountable to the IRS. I also make sure I have faith in their integrity so I don't get taken advantage of.

If you're a numbers cruncher who doesn't feel comfortable and confident stringing words together to write an ad or an article, hire a copywriter.

Whatever it is you don't feel competent to do, or passionate about doing to the best of your ability, you can have done for you. Outsource the pieces of your puzzle that you don't have faith enough to do yourself...and those you have the faith, but not the time, to do yourself.

Work from your faith-based strengths, outsource the rest. That way, every day you'll leap out of bed waiting to get underway again; there will be no more grousing, "Good God, it's morning..." Instead, you'll be cheering, "Good morning, God!"

CHAPTER FIFTEEN

Don't Fear Failure

"Inventor Thomas Edison 'failed' ten thousand times. No one remembers his failures. That's because he never failed himself." — **Kristine M Smith**

"Failure." Sounds like a slap in the face, doesn't it? Toddlers fall down. (Fail!) They get back up. (Victory!)

Failure is part of the learning process. It doesn't minimize who you are or negate what you're working hard to complete. Failures are simply learning opportunities along the way to your success.

Fearing failure is like fearing your next breath. It's gonna happen. You'll live through it. You'll even know something more on the other side of it!

As a copywriter, I want to satisfy—no, I want to **overwhelm with delight**—every client I serve. MOST of the time, I do. And I feel terrible when I don't. But it happens. Does that make me a failure? No.

I either try again, or I refund the money and apologize. But I learn more from every failure than I do from many successes. And the failures—as few and far between as they are— do keep me humble! They remind me that I'm not the answer to **_everybody's_** copywriting needs. I tended to forget that, earlier on, when I was hungrier and experiencing more famine times than I was feast times. I learned that just because I'm struggling financially doesn't mean I should take on every copywriting project I'm invited to quote on. These days I have faith that—as long as I'm working honorably with every client—God will make sure I have enough to get by during times of financial famine. These days I quote ONLY on projects that I'm passionate about myself. That keeps me in good stead with my clients, my Muse and my God.

Think back on the times you failed.

What did you learn?

How did you grow?

What do you know now that you didn't know before the hiccup?

By doing a postmortem on your failures, you'll discover why what you did didn't work and what you need to do to succeed next time.

Toddlers "fall" their way to walking proficiency; they "fall" their way to running proficiency. Older kids "fall" their way to biking proficiency. We don't consider these "experiments in mobility" failures. We smile, hold out our arms, and say, "Good job! Try again!"

You're not failing. You're "falling" forward every time—and forward is where you're headed, so every "try" is a triumph of sorts.

Keep triumphing in spurts until you get where you're going.

CHAPTER SIXTEEN

Don't Fear Success

It's a funny thing. Some people fear success more than they fear failure or mediocrity. Why is that?

From a personal standpoint, among the things I feared were:

- ❖ Not knowing how to take care of my finances
- ❖ Not feeling comfortable talking to strangers (aka "fans," publishers, networking partners, etc.)
- ❖ Not wanting to travel any more
- ❖ Television and radio interviews
- ❖ Being asked to speak to large groups of people
- ❖ Being put on a pedestal and treated like a "celebrity" (gag!)
- ❖ Finding myself so busy that I wouldn't have a life anymore

Being shy and perhaps a bit reclusive (hate that word!) is a curse. Most of the above wouldn't faze a more gregarious person. The funny thing is, as soon as it all started happening, and I **had to** deal with it, most of what I worried about wasn't that big a deal. I mean, I don't have any "stalkers" — and on the rare occasion when someone does treat me like a "celebrity," I quickly kick **that** idea right out from under them! Good golly, Miss Molly, we all put our pants on one leg at a time. Worship your God, not me! Having to "measure up" to the pedestal fans put stars on is a fool's game. The bigger they are, the harder they fall.

What do you fear most about becoming successful? Write them down. Are they *realistic* fears? Remember the acronym F.E.A.R. It stands for "False Evidence Appearing Real." You'll find that most of them are mirages ... and the ones that aren't, you can overcome. I learned to love speaking in public and meeting people of good will who come to hear me speak or read. You will, too. What's not to love about other people's affection for you and what you offer?

Also, write down the many things you **look forward to** about becoming successful in your niche. This list will act as impetus. Tape it on your bathroom mirror. Imagine yourself enjoying them.

Surround yourself with other successful people you genuinely like and respect. That way, you'll learn to accept the idea that you belong among them, and that you are a good fit in their realm.

The biggest "reality check" for me, before I moved to Los Angeles to work in Hollywood, was taking a walking tour of the Paramount and Warner Bros. Studios lots and discovering that all the folks who worked and made a living there were actual human beings—no more "special" (talented, gifted, angelic, determined, whatever my fantasy was) than many of the pro-active folks I'd been hanging around with all my life! The only difference was that they were **already** doing something they considered real special and loved doing it—whether they were driving a tour bus and "talking Hollywood" or making motion pictures and television series; they weren't just daydreaming or thinking about taking the leap of faith that's required to drop everything else and "go for it." They had pursued their passion and ended up where they wanted to be. It wasn't long after this revelation that I joined them and worked with them for thirteen years.

Success isn't something that happens to you; it's something you make happen. Find your passion; pursue it ... and follow where it leads. It isn't rocket science or brain surgery (unless, of course, your passion is rocket science or brain surgery); it's 10 percent inspiration and 90 percent perspiration (pursuit) that puts you into the big leagues.

CHAPTER SEVENTEEN

Love What You Do

"Most men lead lives of quiet desperation and go to the grave with their songs still in them." —**Henry David Thoreau**

If you're like most observers, you nodded in agreement as you read Thoreau's quote above. Take a look around you. How many of the people you know look truly happy, engaged, and energized by the mere fact of their existence and what they're doing with the time they have left before they're shoveled off this mortal coil? It's pathetic, the number of people who seem eager to reach the end of their lives so they can lay down their burdens and rest!

A former pastor of mine, Bill Wolfson—NOT one of the "can't wait to lay my burdens down and be with Jesus"—says often, "I want to die **empty**." What he means is that he wants to leave *nothing undone* that he feels passionate about doing and competent to do—and if he isn't presently competent to do it, he studies and makes himself competent to do it. To him, every day is another day to leap out of the sack and accomplish another task on his bucket list. *If* he has down time, I'd be amazed to know it! He is full of energy, robust, buff. Oh, he's had his wilderness wanderings, his dark nights of the soul, his battles with powers and principalities, as do all human beings…he just never succumbs to them for long. There's a spark in him that refuses to die. He loves what he does and does what he loves.

To enjoy lasting success in any endeavor, finding out what you love to do is crucial, because there will be moments, seasons, and faux "eternities" when loving what you do is the only thing that will keep you moving forward despite setbacks, to-do lists that don't always float your boat, and intervening personalities who set your teeth on edge. Your true north will always be your passion for the course you've set for yourself. You have to love your target so much that no obstacle is too large to obscure your view of it. Sadly, too many people "settle" for a reliable pay check, a secure position (or as secure as any position can be in this wacky world), an "easier"—but deadlier, in the long run—way to make a living. They go along to get along. They won't run the risk of upsetting the apple cart to gain the silver chalice, so quiet desperation sets in.

These people know they can feel better, they know they can leave a legacy of innovation and individual greatness, but … but … but … what they're doing right now leaves them so drained at the end of every day that it takes getting laid off or laid up to re-orient them and get them to start thinking about what they've **always wanted to do** instead of what **they've been doing** for too many years.

Many entrepreneurs are spawned the day the career rug is pulled out from under them, their unemployment benefits run out, and they can't find anyone else willing to hire them. Out of un-quiet desperation, they decide to act—to hang a shingle and start working for themselves, far harder (but happier) than they ever worked for anyone else. And because they're now doing what they love, the long hours don't feel onerous. For the first time in their lives, they're free to set their own sails on the course they've longed to travel most of their lives during the rare quiet moments when they contemplated what life could be like "if only...!"

If the thought of pursuing a career you don't presently have beckons you time after time, your first step is to acknowledge to yourself that you're investing significant energy transforming **other peoples' goals** into realities, not your own.

Here's a litmus test: If the people you're serving at work and/or at home (company, cause, spouse, partner, children, etc.) mean more to you than your own vision of what you'd love to be doing **instead**, you're doing the right thing—and you probably love what you're doing. If not, you're depriving the world of something only YOU can give. You're a unique individual with unique gifts and passions. When you commit whole-heartedly to doing what you love to do, the universe will respond; you'll attract every item and the assistance you need to "make it so."

Someone once asked a wise man where the money would come from to realize his vision. The wise man replied simply, "From wherever it is right now." Ask and you shall receive. Seek and you'll find that you can do what you love to do.

CHAPTER EIGHTEEN
Consider Setbacks Temporary,
Not Reasons to Quit

Successful people don't take "no" for an answer. They don't run out of end runs. They keep on plugging until they find their way around the roadblocks that occur along the way to their goals.

"I give up" and "I can't" aren't in their vocabularies. They map out logical courses, and include tributaries in case the main thoroughfare gets log-jammed.

It is the pioneer spirit—the Lewis and Clark spirit—the pathfinder spirit that calls the shots. Hacking through underbrush, fording rivers, and finding ways to lower prairie schooners into and out of canyons on ropes took ingenuity and elbow grease. Crossing the continent wasn't for the faint-hearted or half-hearted. Neither is pursuing your goals to their terminus and beyond to the next goals.

My dad was a crusty curmudgeon, my mom a genius.

As a youngster, whenever I complained, "I can't…," Dad would explode, "Can't never did nothin'! You CAN, if you just put your mind [or muscle] to it!"

As a teenager, whenever I ran into a roadblock or some heartache, Mom would counsel, "Kris, if this is the worst thing that happens to you in your life, you'll be lucky."

Both statements have served me well. As a late-blooming copywriter and author, I'm living proof that "where there's a will, there's a way." And Mom was right, of course. I've been very, very lucky to have experienced as few traumas in my life as I have; and even though I've experienced quite a few, each one proved to me that I could survive and become stronger and wiser as a result of the storms I encounter along the way. Very little fazes me these days. I just keep going and going and going, like the Energizer Bunny!

When the going gets tough, you just have to keep going. Until you've crossed the finish line, you haven't arrived; it's still out there, waiting for you! Keep moving.

Everybody runs into roadblocks. Ask other people on similar journeys how they overcame the challenges you're facing...or the ones you know you'll be facing down the road.

Roadblocks test your resolve and your mettle. They exercise your ability to think outside the box and find unique solutions. They instill knowledge you wouldn't otherwise have. Consider obstacles worthy "opponents," not impenetrable fortresses. Find your way over, under, around, or through. The universe smiles on guts and guile.

Affirmations:

Eyes on the prize.

Winners never quit.

A thousand-mile journey consists of many steps— not all of them in a straight line.

There is always room at the top.

Today I'll sidestep every obstacle along my path.

CHAPTER NINETEEN

Have a "Significant Other"
Who Inspires You to Keep On Keepin' On

It has been said that if you have three good friends, you have more than your fair share. I hope you have at least three good friends who have your back and who will support your vision on the days when you can't see over the tops of your shoes, because those days **will** stop by to torment you from time to time. You'll need someone at your side (figuratively, at least) who will sing your song whenever you forget the tune.

I had good friends—classmates, teachers, writers, and actors—who kept reminding me that I was not destined for the usual nine-to-five job...and plenty of relatives and acquaintances who kept telling me that I should keep my feet on the ground and get my head out of the clouds. If not for the few who kept singing my song back to me, it might have been completely drowned out by the naysayers ... but as long as I had someone, somewhere, telling me that my passion for stringing words together was leading me to the place where I belonged, I never let myself off the hook. Oh, I complied and got a "real" job...but it was never more than an occupation, a way to keep my head above water on the way to my REAL work.

Napoleon Hill found that all successful people had a significant other who believed in and encouraged them. Simply put, encouragement isn't optional—it's crucial!

If you don't have anyone in your life who acts as a catalyst to your future, find someone. Join groups within your areas of interest; seek out a mentor or coach who can help you build the future you want.

Proactively look for positive, optimistic, knowledgeable, successful people who "have been there and done that," or who know, to a dead certainty, that **you** can. My significant others were Alpha Rossetti and Walter Dobbs, two English teachers; writer and Pulitzer Prize nominee Ted Crail; and actor DeForest Kelley.

These folks were my cheerleaders, mentors, and defenders. They were unpaid "agents" who chatted me up to editors and other power brokers. I still had to do the serious work and hone my skills, but they were the ones who kept *ooh*'ing and *aah*'ing and making me feel as though all I needed was a break and I'd be off and running.

Your significant other may be a spouse, a sister or brother, a schoolmate, an aunt or uncle. It's the people who seem to be always celebrating you—not the ones who seem to be merely tolerating you—that you should listen to. They have no ox to gore with you; they are genuinely on your side and genuinely want to see you succeed so they can applaud and tell everyone "I told you so!" Had I won an Oscar for writing a screenplay, the biggest cheers would have come from other creative people—writers, actors, producers, directors—who know how crucial the words on a page are to the rest of the production. My family would have been proud and happy, but my creative friends would have been DELIRIOUS WITH JOY!

Bask in the praise and belief of others wherever and whenever you find them. Praise and belief are rare and precious. Enjoy the celebration. Hold onto the memories; you'll need them when the road gets rough and dusty. They'll keep you from giving in and giving up.

And one last thing. Verbally appreciate those who celebrate and appreciate you! Let them know what their belief in you means to you. And find out what it is about them—other than their fondness for you—that you should be commending and appreciating. The universe smiles on reciprocity and mutual support. "Thank you," "You're the best!" and "I appreciate you to the moon and back!" goes a long, long way in today's scattered, ships-passing-in-the-night society.

CHAPTER TWENTY

Realize Goals are Magnetic; Genuinely Exude the Right Attitudes and Characteristics to Attract the Essentials You Need to Achieve Them

It has been proven that what you think about causes your immediate environment to respond, to vibrate differently. So don't sit around thinking about what you DON'T want. The universe won't acknowledge the "don't" part of your thought because "don't" doesn't exist in the realm of vibration and matter.

Think about that. Seriously. *Consider the consequences of failing to understand it*. Here's an example:

When you hear a loved one sneeze, you may think or say aloud, "I don't want to catch a cold!" The universe hears, "I...catch a cold," because your emphasis—your strongest emotion and visualization—when you utter the phrase revolves around *catching a cold*!

Always verbalize your goals using positive words. Instead of, "I don't want to catch a cold," confirm to the universe (and visualize it), "My immune system is vigorous!"

The same concept works with goals. Instead of allowing yourself to think negatively—e.g., "I'll always be poor," "I'll never get ahead," or "Money burns a hole in my pocket the minute I get it,"—direct your attention to the outcome you DO want. "Every day I'm putting more money into my bank account," "I'm saving 2 percent more than I did last month," and "I'm becoming a conscientious steward of the money that is coming my way these days."

Turn your fears into affirmations, and then allow your affirmations to guide your path and direct your steps.

You attract what you **genuinely**—deep down inside—believe you deserve. If you're struggling now, spend some time thinking about what you've been communicating to the universe. Has your output been positive, loving, friendly, hopeful, giving...or has it been fearful, grasping, mean-spirited, or in any other way unhelpful or harmful? If you take the time to analyze and deconstruct when things began going south, you'll often find a correlation between the status of your inner thoughts, your outer actions, and the results you see manifesting in your life. It's no fun to think about that, but it is often true.

What does this mean to you career-wise and in other ways? Love what you're after. Address its attainment in positive terms. Speak and think about what you **do** want. Train yourself to think and speak in terms of what's *possible* rather than what's most common or most likely. Evict the naysayer from your cranium.

Attract what you want by focusing on what you love about it. True love wins others' hearts and minds. Envision what the world will look like when you get where you're going and "act as if" you already have it. Before you know it, you probably will!

CHAPTER TWENTY-ONE

Be Positive and Passionate

Compare and contrast how you feel and act on different days.

None of us are immune to "low days," when we feel like grousing, swearing, and kicking things—hopefully nothing with nerve endings. On days like these, your best bet is to isolate yourself as much as possible, or if you simply MUST be on display, at least announce that you have one nerve left and you're praying that no one gets on it today. Your announcement alone usually causes everyone to scatter—unless they positively, absolutely MUST interact with you on an urgent matter—which is a good thing!

On "high days," we feel "all's well with the world" and that we could kiss a prince, a pauper, and a toad with equal parts of love and compassion. On days like these, do your best to consciously "memorize" the feeling. It's when you're in this "zone" that you can be most effective and do the most good for the greatest number of people (or animals, or whatever your particular passion is). If you memorize it well enough, it becomes easier to summon it on the in-between days when you need a little extra "boost" to keep on keepin' on.

The good news is that when you're doing what you truly love to do your naturally "high" days become more numerous and your low days become nearly as rare as hens' teeth. Positivity and passion vibrate at higher frequencies, and "an object in motion tends to stay in motion"—the higher you vibrate, the better you feel. Your endorphins get in on the act and flood you with feel-good hormones. Your work feels like play and your co-workers become playmates and cheerleaders. Making things happen becomes a fun puzzle instead of a wearisome battle.

Positive, passionate people smile a lot. They joke with, cajole, and recruit equally-positive compatriots. Although they're deadly serious about getting things done—reaching their goals— they're equally serious about having fun and building "fond bonds" along the way. Because, let's face it, working long hours isn't always a laugh-a-minute; sometimes it's a tedious, protracted battle. Positive people want other positive people in the foxhole with them.

On your way to wherever it is you're headed, remember to build "fond bonds" with the people you rely on and who rely on you. It can be lonely at the top (if you ever manage to get there all by yourself—HIGHLY UNLIKELY!) unless you've recruited dedicated, knowledgeable, fun people and encouraged fellowship among them.

Have play dates. Go on outings that have nothing to do with your entrepreneurial or other goals. Find ways to encourage and honor your partners' positivity and passion. By doing this, you'll find the hard days easier to get through and the happy days happier than they would otherwise be, because you'll be sharing them with genuine friends...

CHAPTER TWENTY-TWO

Foster a Success-Conscious Mindset

Success-conscious people read different publications than other people. I'm not talking only about *Forbes*, *Business Week*, *The Wall Street Journal*, *Entrepreneur*, *Inc.* and other business-type venues, although these publications are on many reading lists. Success-conscious people also read about winning, negotiating, spirituality, compromising (and when not to), and psychology. In doing so, they run across—and usually run into (at conventions and other venues)—the movers and shakers that dot the landscape of the rich and famous, whether it's Bishop TD Jakes, Dr. Phil, Anthony Robbins, Zig Ziglar, Brendan Burchard, Donald Trump, Warren Buffett, Bill Gates, Newt Gingrich, Mitt Romney, Oprah Winfrey, Steve Forbes, or any other of a number of successful folks.

It behooves you to make a point of "hanging with" the successful people you have access to that you most admire. (I repeat: the ones you most admire! There are rich people everywhere; you don't have to hang with the ones who upset your stomach. You won't learn anything if you're in the bathroom the whole time because you can't endorse their politics, their religion, or their narrow, or too-broad-minded attitudes.)

If you weren't "to the manor born"—if success is, or will be, a culture shock to you—it's a great idea to find ways to rub elbows with success-conscious people because watching how they interact with their peers and audiences is good to know. One way to get your feet wet is to attend conferences where successful people will be speaking. Many of these events offer Q & A sessions. But even if you don't ask a question, listening to the answers the speakers give other attendees, and their attitudes as they answer, will offer a boatload of information and insights into the mindset of successful people. First of all, you may be surprised to discover how down to earth many of them are. You may also be horrified to discover how self-important some of them are. The self-important ones are NOT good role models; avoid them. Trust me on this!

Prepare for these events by reading the books the speakers have written beforehand. The information helps you formulate questions that aren't already answered in their books, and the approachable ones will recognize you for your ability to ask questions they haven't already answered hundreds of times before *ad nauseum*. This will help you stand out so that, if you get a chance to rub elbows later, they will remember you as "someone special" and may take extra time with you.

Being in the right place at the right time isn't just a matter of luck. Success-minded people make much of their own luck by placing themselves at venues where they have an increased likelihood of meeting someone who can help them reach the next step on their journey.

Success-conscious people recognize astuteness, enthusiasm, and competency quickly, so by essaying these attributes, you place yourself where you're most likely to be noticed by someone who can benefit from what you know and do, just as you can benefit from what they know and do. In the business world, synergies and partnerships happen all the time from just such "serendipitous" (or pre-arranged) encounters.

By developing a success-conscious mindset, you'll find yourself spotting opportunities for growth and refinement. Just as you suddenly notice "your" vehicle model everywhere around you just after you've bought new wheels, you will begin to recognize opportunities to interact with other success-minded people wherever you find them. And you'll often develop a sixth sense about **where** you need to go off the beaten path **to** find them.

Successful people are everywhere you look. Bless them somehow, if you can, without expectation. Help them reach a goal, make a contact or solve a problem. One time at Warner Bros late at night, I came across a Mazerati owner in the parking garage who was beside himself, looking under the hood. I stopped to ask what the problem was. He said he needed a jump. I pulled out my cables and brought his Mazerati roaring back to life from my beat up little Mazda's battery. He gushed, "Thank you so much. Here's my card. Anything you want, anything! Just ask!" I asked for *nada*. Who was he? The screenwriter of PATRIOT GAMES!

CHAPTER TWENTY-THREE

Recognize the True Value of Your Goals

When focusing on our goals, we often put blinders on and can't see the forest for the trees. We agonize over every setback, concentrate on every small detail, and completely lose our perspective. Doing so leads us to believe that our success is crucial *only to ourselves* and our significant others. We commiserate quietly late at night as we sit at our desks busting our butts to make this thing work right so we don't lose our shirts in our attempt to build an amazing career and life. It's just so easy to become self-absorbed and myopic. No one else knows what we're going through, so we think we're the only ones our success will affect.

Thinking this way is a huge handicap!

My goal to become an author and copywriter became—for a time—all about me. It became about bringing enough in to keep my head above water, about establishing and proving myself, about finding ways to get the word out as inexpensively as I could, since I didn't have much start-up capital and zero budget for marketing. Thinking this way, of course, helped me focus on my own survival. I did exactly what I had to do to get this far in my career. It took herculean effort and blinders-on focus.

But now that I'm farther along on my journey, I've come back to the real reason I decided to take this trip all along. My own survival as a full-time professional copywriter and author is a pale and puny thing when I compare it to the hundreds of other people who would have lost had I failed or bailed. Because, after all is said and done, it's the people I serve—the folks who need what I know and do and seek me out—who are equal partners and beneficiaries. Writing to please myself is a hobby and a pastime. I love stringing words together. But writing to further someone else's cause, or tout their excellent products or services, is a SERVICE that not just anyone else can provide to them. The clients I have and keep know this; they've learned it the hard way. You get what you pay for. If your budget is anemic, you can hire an anemic writer, but your sales won't be as robust. If you pay a writer who knows what they're doing and charges adequately for their expertise, the payoff of your trust is usually skyrocketing sales or more money for your cause, a win-win situation.

So these days my "struggles" as a writer (feast or famine, famine or feast—the life rhythm of a creative!) rarely seem to be about me. I get up every morning, not so much to make money, but to make some other entrepreneur's day by blowing them away with copy that they would get nowhere else for even ten times the price I charge.

I love what I do; I love the client feedback I get.

I've never taken drugs, but my job and the wonderful feedback I get from clients make me so "high" on a daily basis that I don't think anything, manufactured or natural, could even compete!

When **you** recognize the true value of **your** goals, absolutely nothing will keep you from attaining them.

So take the blinders off. Make a poster or a banner of what the world will get when you reach the goals you've set for yourself. Get out of your own head and your own skin and realize that **this isn't about you**. Not really. It's about the legacy you want to leave when the curtain closes on your life.

You have work to do that will thrill you even as it blesses the socks off other people. Get going. Too many people still have their socks on! They're waiting for you!

CHAPTER TWENTY-FOUR

In Conclusion:

You Were Born to Do What You Love to Do!

DON'T SETTLE FOR LESS!

The reason I undertook this new endeavor was to encourage **you** to find out what you love to do, and then find ways to do it for a living.

Sad fact: It took me fifty seven (57!!!) years to decide to "go for it" and hang my shingle as a full-time copywriter, and fifty years to publish my first book. I *do not* want it to take you that long!

The steps I've laid out here detail what Napoleon Hill called the "common denominators" of all self-made millionaires. They work. But they only work when you and I work them.

You were made of stern stuff. You have a dream, a goal. If you aren't yet doing what you know you were born to do, here's plenty of proof that it isn't too late:

- Leonardo da Vinci was drawing sketches in his sixties.
- Frank McCourt, the author of *Angela's Ashes,* penned his first manuscript in his sixties.
- Ronald Reagan became President of the United States at age sixty-one.
- Golf legend Sam Snead won the Par 3 Tournament when he was sixty-one.
- Mahatma Gandhi marched 240 miles in twenty-four days with his followers at the age of sixty-one to make their own salt from the sea in defiance of Britain's colonial laws and taxes.
- William Jennings Bryan battled the teaching of evolution in schools at the age of sixty-one.
- Leo Tolstoy wrote novels in his seventies.
- Benjamin Franklin played an instrumental role in drafting and signing the Declaration of Independence at an advanced age and signed the U.S. Constitution at eighty-one years old.
- Grandma Moses was eighty-six when she painted her first picture.

- Michelangelo was sculpting in his eighties.
- Winston Churchill was active and productive until his death at ninety years old.
- George Burns remained active, funny, and fully employed until he was over one hundred!

So jump in with both feet and 100 percent of your heart, mind, and spirit. Keep smiling.

Persist. Persuade. Perspire.

Insist. Inquire. Inspire.

Note from Publisher: Cheryl Haynes

If you have enjoyed this book, please consider the following titles by Kristine M. Smith:

• *Floating Around Hollywood.* Always amusing and often downright hilarious collection of reminiscences by Kris Smith spotlighting her adventures as a "floating secretary" in Tinsel Town.

A.C. Lyles, legendary producer and goodwill ambassador to the entertainment industry at *Paramount Pictures*, writes, *"Kris Smith's entertainment industry career reads like a sitcom."*

DeForest Kelley's back cover comment is: *"A fast-paced book, full of laughter, written with comedic skill. It's a delightful read."*

• *Let No Day Dawn That the Animals Cannot Share*

Art by Emese Dian
Foreword by DeForest Kelley
"A mostly-serious collection of Smith's animal "pros-e-try" which will clutch passionately at the reader's heart and spirit. The book spotlights humankind's deeply-rooted emotional, ethical and spiritual bond to the animal kingdom, wild and domestic, and then identifies areas in which we have fallen,

painfully and dangerously, short regarding our stewardship of scores of precious and irreplaceable fellow creatures. Get out a box of tissues for this one."

• DeForest Kelley: A Harvest of Memories: My Life and Times with a Remarkable Gentleman Actor

Garnering 5-star reviews at on-line bookstores everywhere.

The actor best-remembered as a science fiction icon is recaptured in word and deed in this affectionate and affecting personal memoir. The author writes,

"We need honorable role models who do not disappoint once the camera lens turns away. De was my friend, but he was also my hero—one of very few heroes whose durability was sorely tested, yet found to be utterly reliable. I wrote this book to show how deeply De influenced my life—and to remind you, his fans and friends, how seamlessly and comfortably he fit into yours. For the millions of fans who did not have the chance to meet De up close and personal, this is your gateway . . . Enter, heartstrings attached!"

If you know DeForest Kelley solely through his 50-year acting career in motion pictures and television, this book will become a treasured keepsake. For true fans of all ages.

The Enduring Legacy of DeForest Kelley

DeForest Kelley's former personal assistant Kristine M. Smith has compiled the memories and reminiscences of fans and friends whose lives were blessed and changed forever by the career or kindness of the late actor who portrayed Dr. Leonard McCoy in the original Star Trek series. All who contributed to the tome have realized the immense impact that the iconic "Bones" has had on their lives and careers. Smith reveals that, "Kelley's enduring legacy includes fans who continue to boldly go where few have gone before, making a difference every step of the way."

Serval Son: Spots and Stripes Forever

If you have ever wondered what it's like to own—and be owned by—a wild pet, get ready to experience it in ways you will never forget.

The author, Kristine M. Smith, does not advocate the keeping of wild pets, especially wild cats, wild dogs and simians. To the contrary, for the many reasons she explains and has endured, she is opposed to wild animal ownership for most people. The commitment is brutal, the risks enormous, the memories indelible (good and bad).

But there are times when the urge to adopt a wild animal seems uncontrollable—part of your destiny. If you've felt the tug, this book will

**introduce you to what you'll be getting into.
Look before you leap.**

Praise for SERVAL SON

"Kris Smith is a warrior with a true love and respect for all animals. I love her."—Tippi Hedren (from the FOREWORD), The ROAR Foundation, Shambala Preserve (shambala.org)

"If someone in Hollywood doesn't option this story to make a movie of it, they're asleep at the switch. SERVAL SON ranks right up there with MARLEY AND ME."—Stephanie Ealy, ALLVOICES Anchor, Tacoma WA